THE POWER OF ACTION

11 Strategies for Achieving Your Goals and Living Your Best Life

Chinedu Nkwoemeka

DISCLAIMER

We are not financial or legal advisors. The content provided is for educational purposes and does not take the place of financial or legal advice from a professional. We have tried to ensure that the content provided in this book is accurate and helpful to our readers at publishing time. However, this is not an exhaustive treatment of the subjects. We assume no liability for losses or damages because of the information provided. You are responsible for your choices, actions, and results, and you should consult a professional for your specific publishing and disclaimer questions and needs.

Printed by (Author)

Published in the Federal Republic of Nigeria

First Printing Edition, 2023
ISBN: 9798376760963

TABLE OF CONTENTS

Title Page

Copyright

Table of Contents

Preface

Phase One - **A Better Way to Live**

Chapter One - **The Power of Honesty**

Chapter Two - **Think Bigger**

Chapter Three - **Use Your Imagination**

Chapter Four - **Making Personal Sacrifices?**

Chapter Five - **Take Smart Risks**

Chapter Six - **Lifelong Learning**

Chapter Seven - **Focus on the Fundamentals**

Phase Two - **The Darker Side**

Chapter Eight - **Conflict Resolution: Navigating Difficult Relationships**

Chapter Nine - **The Art of Prioritization: How to Make the Most of Your Time**

Chapter Ten - **Investing for Success: Maximizing Your Life**

Conclusion

Appendix

Acknowledgments

About The Author

Notes

Quotable

PREFACE

Everyone has dreams and goals to achieve to live a complete life. Many people get what they want, and many more don't come close to achieving their goals and getting what they want. What is the critical difference between these people? Is it their habits or their character, skill level, luck, or destiny, or are they communicating with some type of higher power?

You may have all these valid questions, yet it's simpler; it's their actions that make them who they are.

Everyone has aspirations, goals, and habits. The difference is the actions they take. Good decisions and lifestyle choices; are actions that can make you level up faster than the average person.

Every action creates a reaction, this law holds everywhere every time. Every time you make a particular action you are creating an event, which causes a sequence of reactive events in motion that will lead to a specific outcome. So, if you want to change your outcome, you only have to change your actions. It's that simple. This law holds for everyone everywhere. What separates you, the most successful and influential person from the rest is that you take the right action at the right time

"Today is the tomorrow of yesterday" - Me

1 How can you determine the right action to take every single time? That is the trillion-dollar question. Even the best chess masters could not make the best moves at every turn. These strategies are the core focus of his book.

There are seven mainline strategies and three other strategies that you will learn to become the person you want to be, regardless of your current occupation or experience, or education. You may already know these rules and you may already apply them. This book will only allow you to remember them. Use these rules; the rules work because the laws are universal.

"Ideas are worth a dime a dozen, but people who put them into action are priceless." - Mary Kay Ash

You will understand if you keep an open mind. the right way is the hard way, develop a deeper understanding of the ideas in this book by putting them into practice. The closer an object is to the light, the darker the shadow.

Is this book for you? It's for the person who wants transcendence and wants to discover who he is and who he deserves to be, irrespective of age, gender, race, occupation, or net worth. This is one of the greatest books in the world; the power is in your hands today.

CHINEDU NKWOEMEKA

05th February 2023

Phase One - A better way to live

Me: Why am I me?

Her: You are who you are because of a combination of factors, including your genetics, your environment, your experiences, and your thoughts and beliefs.

Me: if I am me because of these things, then to change me, I only have to change these things, how do I change these things?

Her: Here are some ways you may change these things.

Genetics: While it is not possible to change your genetics directly, you can take steps to improve your overall health and well-being, which can have an impact on your genetic expression. This might include eating a healthy diet, getting regular exercise, and getting enough sleep.

Environment: You can take steps to improve your environment in ways that support your well-being. This might include decluttering your living space, finding ways to reduce stress and increase relaxation, and spending time in nature.

Experiences: Seek out new and challenging experiences that allow you to learn and grow. This might include trying new hobbies, traveling to new places, or volunteering for a cause you are passionate about.

Thoughts: Practice mindfulness and positive thinking by paying attention to your thoughts and working to replace negative or unhelpful thoughts with more positive ones.

Beliefs: Reflect on your beliefs and consider whether they are helping or hindering your personal growth. If necessary, seek out new perspectives and information that can help you develop a more nuanced and balanced understanding of the world.

The way is action because action creates change, after the change comes results, a dynamic is created which creates the desired ideas.

CHAPTER ONE - THE POWER OF HONESTY

Written in this chapter is the spiritual way of life, this is the way of mastery and control over your circumstances. Any other knowledge contrary to this chapter is false. If you seek the truth you will find it and you will find life. This is the way that all great men and women follow, if they deviate from this path, they observe this and correct it. Follow this way and you will discover it for yourself. The power of honesty is not power over other people, it is power over yourself, your body, and your spirit.

"True statements are 1's. False statements are 0's." - Me

In accepting ultimate freedom and happiness, there are a few actions that can hinder the true self-actualization of many people who would have become successful. The most common of these is dishonesty.

"People lie because they are afraid. If you have no fear, you wouldn't need to lie to anyone."

Why do people lie? To cover up the truth. Living is truth, to cover the truth is to hate life. Lying is a weakness. Truth is life, life is the way, and the way is strength. Lying is learned. It is not natural; you may have learned it, and you can unlearn it.

"Lack of integrity has caused many people to never rise above."

2 A narcissistic person says, "I don't care what people think about me" That is a false statement. We are social beings; we do better as a team. Nobody wants to be on a team of liars. Dishonesty hinders people from living a fulfilling life and getting what they want. In reverse, honesty is the key to a great life.

Lying tends to come back to haunt the liar. Create a visual representation of what you do to yourself if you lie. You will understand. The path to freedom is in front of you.

Thinking honestly is the way of winning! Lying weakens and drains the mental energy of its victims. Chronic liars caught in a deep web of lies; are standing under a tree full of venomous web-spinning spiders. They have become "faux". The real "person" is dying, while the fake "person" is far from his true being. There is hope, however.

A ++ reputation for honesty is more powerful than you may think. Your honesty may offend people, and respect is better than pleasing people in the short term. Thinking honestly is the true way of winning.

Dishonesty is always the way to lose, chronic liars will become empty souls. In contrast, honest people have high moral standards and this attracts people to them. Be careful, all smiling faces are not honest and all frowning faces are not unhappy. A great leader will tell the difference. People usually lie because of fear of failure or embarrassment. There is much more to gain from thinking honestly than dishonestly.

3 Notice that dishonesty is not a criminal offense, this is why it is much more prevalent. You have a choice.

"Truth never damages a cause that is just." - Mahatma Gandhi

Waste no time being defensive and close-minded, accept this truth, it is better, to be honest. It is the right time now to start thinking honestly. If you have been a liar in the past, honesty is the first change you should make. A person who doesn't have control over her tongue should not have a tongue. A dishonest individual tells lies with more than a tongue.

"Honesty is the first chapter in the book of wisdom." - Thomas Jefferson

True statements are 1's, and false statements are 0's. There are few things more dangerous to your self-fulfillment than lying.

"The most powerful force in the universe is love." - Albert. E

To start applying the power of honesty to your own life, you may keep a journal and write down your thoughts and actions every day. Be honest with yourself about your motivations and feelings. Reflect on your experiences and how honesty has played a role in them. You can also try practicing radical honesty with others, being open and transparent about your thoughts and feelings without fear of judgment.

Remember, honesty is the foundation of all great relationships and endeavors.

"Honesty is a cornerstone of all success, without which confidence and ability to perform shall cease to exist." - Mary Kay Ash

Embrace honesty in your life and unlock new opportunities that lead you to a happier, more fulfilling path.

This is the spiritual way and the first strategy.

CHAPTER TWO - THINK BIGGER

"Go big or go home; there is no alternative."- Me

Written in this chapter is the mental way of abundance. Everything comes from a source. The source is abundant. All great men and women know this and they all tap into this abundant source. There is no knowledge contrary to this. It is an absolute fact that the way of contentment is to think bigger. Following this way, is the way of self-realization. You will discover the limitless power that comes from this way. You will experience abundance which comes from the knowledge of the source.

In the quest to get what you want, should you give it your all? Yes. Mediocrity is poverty, and it is more dangerous to be poor in the mind than to be poor in cash. A person poor in cash but rich in the mind may not remain poor for long, and a simpleton may be eternally poor.

Encourage the idea that you should want more; you can achieve so much more with your heart and soul and set your sights on lofty targets. Think Bigger, think of excellence, and always aim high. To get what you want, aim high, then aim higher.

"Think big; think disruptive. Execute with full passion." - Jack Ma

Successful free people expand themselves by thinking bigger, they put in the required effort and leverage it, they think honestly, they think of only what they want, they get started, and they usually always finish what they start. They allow faith to control their mind, they think they can, they are practical, and they know they don't have to be exceptional to start, and that is why they can get what they want or become who they want to be, they save themselves and save others. This is an accurate thinking process.

People who do not wait for an opportunity and seek it instead, people who start when required and make sure they finish. They have gained control over their lives and they use it for their best interest. They have saved themselves and now seek the highest purpose of saving others.

You may not feel unique and you may not feel like an extraordinary genius, this is irrelevant. People tend to become a product of their environment, we tend to apply the knowledge we have with the energy we possess, and acquire experiences and skills in our lifetime. Everybody has this potential for greatness. The people who become great are remarkable because they are regular human beings who found out what they wanted early enough and focused on it. When you start focusing on the present moment, you will find a unique solution to every problem.

You can be greater than you previously thought, you can do greater things than you know, and you can get what you want. The strategy is thinking only about the things you want and not paying any attention to the things you do not want. You can achieve anything, believe this and live with this idea. Think honestly always and allow yourself to think bigger. Everything is possible.

When you think of an idea, that idea will develop into a thought, and thoughts usually become reality when **action** is taken on those thoughts. It's also more accurate to constantly focus on your strengths and your limitless potential. Anything that can be done can be improved upon. This is the mental way of life.

To start thinking bigger, set challenging goals for yourself and find honest ways to achieve them. Seek out new opportunities and be open to new experiences. Surround yourself with like-minded individuals who inspire and support you. And always remember to stay true to your ethical values and beliefs.

"Think bigger. Think differently. Take risks. Embrace change. Don't be afraid to fail. And never settle for less than you deserve."

By adopting this mindset, you are opening yourself up to unlimited possibilities and setting yourself on a path to achieving your greatest dreams.

Remember, it is always the right time to start thinking bigger and reaching for the stars. As the famous quote goes, "If you can dream it, you can do it."

So out there think bigger, strive for excellence, and never settle for less. You have the power within you, to create a life of abundance and fulfillment, and it all starts with the way you think. Remember, "The only limits in life are the ones you set for yourself."

"The most dangerous poison is the feeling of achievement. The antidote is to think what can be done better tomorrow." - Ingvar Kamprad

Encourage yourself to new heights and always strive for improvement. You will achieve greatness and create the life you have always dreamed of because you can become truly exceptional.

This is the mental way and the second strategy.

CHAPTER THREE - USE YOUR IMAGINATION

*"And the Lord said, Behold, the people are one, and they all have one language; and this they begin to do: and now nothing will be restrained from them, which they have **imagined** to do." - The book of Genesis 11:6*

Introduction

Written in this chapter is a strategy based on the philosophical standpoint of intuition. It calls upon a person to discover that which may already exist or not. It is an aggressive strategy, and it is usually naturally employed when one is forced to use it. Where there is comfort, imagination is usually rare. However, you may push yourself beyond your comfort zones and use the power of imagination. This is the way of the infinite. A trained mind will allow you to see no limits in this way, showing you solutions to make you adapt to the new realities, you will easily understand this and reach your full limitless potential, and you will find great wisdom through this way. There is no knowledge contrary to this way. Notice the great creative achievements that have come from imagination, especially when it becomes necessary for survival. You will discover this truth for yourself when you begin to apply this way. The way of intuition.

The power of the human brain and the importance of imagination

4 The human brain is a marvel of evolution, capable of processing vast amounts of information, making complex decisions, and even imagining entirely new worlds.

This ability to imagine new things, as we all know, has taken humanity from eating cold food to creating artificial intelligence. The journey to freedom is like a map leading us through the unexplored universe of our creativity.

What is Creative Intelligence?

Creative intelligence refers to the ability to generate and apply novel ideas and solutions to problems. It involves the capacity to think creatively and to use one's imagination to come up with new and innovative ideas. There are various ways to foster creative intelligence, including;

- Engaging in creative activities
- Developing a growth mindset.
- Seeking out diverse experiences and perspectives.

Some people may be naturally more inclined towards creative thinking, and it is a skill that everyone can develop and strengthen over time through practice and effort. Success is a testament to the power of imagination and the value of pursuing your passions with creativity and determination.

"Creativity is more important than knowledge." - Albert. E

The Value of Creative Thinking

It is common for people to believe that knowledge is power, and this is not always the case. They may have formed this belief from their own experiences, or they may have been told by friends and family, this is a misconception. Knowledge is rarely powerful unless it is applied creatively.

You have been born with enough creative energy and vision to last ten lifetimes. Children are complete freethinkers; their instinct is to explore, and they always think about new things. Adults have greater vision and they may also be more disciplined, however, they may have also allowed their minds to become clouded and they may have created completely fictitious limits. The world usually craves change, imagination is a dynamic power!

Most people have experienced some form of formal education. The right type of education can encourage creativity. Having strong memory and analytical skills can certainly help foster creativity, additionally being able to imagine new ideas and combine them with old ones, creates greater innovations.

The Importance of Thinking Outside the Box

The system rewards those who can understand facts and apply them. The modern capitalistic world follows a natural order; the natural order operates the same way it has operated for millions of years, and that is–those who apply the best ideas successfully, win. In the natural world, it is rarely those with the most knowledge who are rewarded. Rather, it is more commonly those who have the best ideas and the wisdom to apply them successfully who tend to thrive especially when they possess the understanding to make other people understand and believe in their ideas. All the most incredible people know this and they have been thriving; the unfortunate ones suffer at the bottom.

Since the times of the earliest ancestors, when an intelligent primate used a long stick to pluck a fruit out of reach, while some other primates may have died of hunger and complaints, the world's most significant theories, athletic fits, businesses, songs, inventions, art, and literature are because of imagination. These are all great ideas that never existed until someone had the intuition, tested them, created them, and applied them.

"Throughout history, imagination has led to some of the most significant theories, inventions, art, literature, and businesses."

The Role of Creativity in Problem-Solving

_5_ There is a lot of information on the World Wide Web. Creative new ideas are more important today because they give you an advantage. The world loves to experience innovation. It is no longer surprising for someone to grow a single idea from nothing to be worth billions of dollars in a few years or for entire industries to be completely turned around by a simple concept; more recently Blockchain, Streaming, and AI.

People with great intuition vs people without. To develop your intuitiveness, you have to constantly use your imagination; you have to control your mind and understand that this world is only the output, your mind creates what you see; the more you use your intuition and creative imagination, the more efficient you get at using it and unlocking a limitless mindset. You can train your mind to be more creative and powerful. You are free to use this power, exercise it more, and get better at using it, even beyond what you thought was possible.

True knowledge comes from knowing what is important. The most successful people are those who function creatively when everyone else follows rigid thinking patterns. Imagination creates power, and this is based on objective evidence. In medieval times, people were quite ignorant, so those with any form of specialized knowledge became powerful, hence the saying (Knowledge is power). Even then, it wasn't always so.

Imagination and creativity are important. Many humans hardly ever think creatively; work-life takes them from one repetitive task to another. This way is a poor way to live.

The Connection Between Creativity and Happiness

Successful people do think differently. They make time for exercise, spiritual activities, and creative thinking. They make time each day to be creative, we as humans are natural creatives, and that is who we become.

The power of imagination and freedom of emotion is limitless, and it is free! You don't need to buy a book or attend classes to get it; it is there for you to use. Use your imagination. **Close your eyes so you can now see clearly.** Allow the ideal "you" to come into full being and presence; the real "you". Use your imagination. Use your intuition.

This is the philosopher's way, it is the third strategy.

Chapter Summary

- Use your imagination and creativity.
- Your intuition is correct it rewards innovation greatly.
- You are limitless and all-powerful.

In the next chapter, you will learn…

1. How to leave your comfort zone.
2. Why you should make sacrifices.
3. How abundance comes through sacrifice.

CHAPTER FOUR - MAKING PERSONAL SACRIFICES?

On your journey to transcending success, you will find yourself in positions where you may have to make sacrifices. Do not fret when you come across these situations. You can make the correct decisions. Be at peace with yourself and consider what is at stake. Look at your choices practically, without any attachments, sentiment, or entitlement, you will be able to make the correct and accurate decisions. When you have made a decision do not quickly go back on it. Enter the sacrifice with boldness, this is how you will learn. All sacrifice has to be personal.

<u>6</u> There is a route from point A to point B. There is only so much time available, and you will have to carry only those essential things. Leave some old habits behind, old friends, a relationship, or an old neighborhood.

You will have to make sacrifices to get out of your comfort zone; you may leave your current home and head to a new and unknown country, learn, and acquire life-changing experiences. Leaving your comfort zone and taking risks are part of the sacrifices you have to make to achieve your goals and reach your full potential. You will also focus on activities that are productive and contribute to your goals.

You should let negative people go and stop wasting your energy with them, let toxic and unproductive people go. Why waste your time and energy on things that don't benefit you or contribute to your goals? It's always better to let go of these types of people. Quit while you can and stop **doing unimportant things.** Think carefully. Negative habits come in various forms and they don't improve your life. It would be wiser to spend your time learning. To gain abundance, shouldn't you focus on the things that matter and walk away from the things that do not matter?

Instead of trying to do everything yourself, learn to delegate and save your time and energy. Get professional help instead of wasting time trying to do unimportant things on your own.

Making sacrifices such as changing cities, switching jobs, or starting your own business will be difficult and may be necessary to achieve your goals; this is a sacrifice of comfort and a search for opportunity. You will have to make sacrifices to get what you want. Can you embrace the challenges and sacrifices that come with pursuing your dreams? Are you willing to stay out of your comfort zone? Are you prepared to take that giant leap to get what you want? Say yes to all of these.

Most people want a better life, they want more money, and they want more time for themselves. Still, they refuse to do what is required, some are only distracted while some genuinely don't know what to do, which leads to the chapter on educating yourself. Shouldn't you spend more time getting what you want? Written in this book are practical strategies that will help you achieve personal growth and self-improvement through self-awareness, self-discovery, and self-mastery. Understanding your limitations and weaknesses will allow you to see how small they are and will let you identify areas for improvement and turn them into strengths. If you do not know your strengths how can you use them?

Making sacrifices can help you uncover new opportunities and potential that you may not have been aware of before. Are you letting the opinions of people who've never done it before or aren't as successful as you want to hold you back from pursuing your dreams and goals? If so, you have to stop now. Stop procrastinating, stop dawdling, get ready quickly, and go. You'll learn so much more from real experiences.

"Great achievement is usually born of great sacrifice and is never the result of selfishness." - Napoleon Hill

For *charitable* reasons. Malala is a Pakistani activist for female education and the youngest Nobel Prize laureate. At a young age, she sacrificed her safety and comfort to speak out against the Taliban's prohibition on the education of girls in her native Swat Valley. Despite facing threats and violence, Malala persisted in her activism and eventually gained international recognition for her efforts. Her story is an inspiring example of the power of making sacrifices in the pursuit of a greater cause.

You may never know the full extent of your potential or what you're capable of achieving until you take the risk and make sacrifices. This is why you should make sacrifices; giving up is the first and only step to failure. Every positive sacrifice you make will ultimately contribute to your overall success and bring you closer to achieving your goals. Imagine you want to move into a new house, expand your business, get a graduate degree, build your body, and do something you've never done before, maybe you want to do all of these.

How do you achieve all these things? Maybe you start working on one of these goals, maybe you list all the things you want, then start tackling the most important task first. Each task requires a sacrifice. You may begin by sacrificing time and pleasure to join a gym program, then sacrificing comfort to leave below your means, and then sacrificing even more time to research and write a business plan. Believe it, you are already generating momentum. Naturally, making sacrifices requires guts and control over yourself, everyone can learn how to do it. It only takes a conscious effort.

You may have to make a positive sacrifice to gain an advantage; no matter how big or small, do what is required to get what you want. Seek abundance.

This is the warrior's way, it is the fourth strategy.

Things you want	Things you don't want	Personal sacrifices to be made	Action Step
Complete Self-Control and Self-Mastery	Mental, Emotional, and Physical Weakness	Time to Train. Cutting off unnecessary activities, I do for pleasure.	I will give two hours every day to train my body and mind.

Use this format to make your sacrifices.

Chapter Summary

- You have to be able to detach from anything.
- No one can tell you the whole experience; only you can experience it for yourself.

- Abundance comes through selflessness and service to others.

In the next chapter, you will learn...

1. Tips for taking smart risks and achieving success in your own life.
2. The importance of flexibility and adaptability in risk-taking.
3. The benefits of taking smart risks in pursuit of personal and professional growth.

CHAPTER FIVE - TAKE SMART RISK

"He who is not courageous enough to take risks will accomplish nothing in life." - Muhammad Ali

In this chapter, you may come to understand the truth about living and you may discover it is likely not what it seems. This strategy highlights the importance of smart risks, and why and how you should take smart risks. Ambition is complimented with discipline, adventure is complimented with romance. This chapter is a word of wisdom, to encourage the now settled spirit to be faithful even more now, and be willing to risk the unknown and step into the void. The mastery of self is necessary to be able to take smart risks. You will understand these things through training and you will discover the true meaning for yourself.

Risk-taking is an integral part of the journey toward achieving your goals and living a fulfilling life. It is necessary to step outside your comfort zone, try new things, and challenge yourself to grow and improve. However, it is important to understand that taking intelligent risks means being measured and controlled, and not engaging in reckless or irresponsible behavior.

In 2020, Nigerian youths took a smart risk by protesting against the corrupt police organization known as SARS. We knew we could face violence and persecution from the authorities, yet we were willing to take this risk because we believed it was important to stand up for our rights and to fight against corruption. Our efforts paid off, as the federal government agreed to disband SARS and reform the police force.

Another example of a successful risk-taker is RM, a rapper from South Korea. RM, whose real name is Kim Nam-Joon, initially pursued a career in the arts as a theater actor. However, he eventually discovered his passion for music and decided to pursue a career as a rapper, even though rap was not a popular genre in South Korea at the time. RM took the risk of following his passion and it paid off. He is now the leader of the globally successful K-pop group BTS and has released several successful solo albums. In addition to his music career, RM has also become a respected public figure and is known for his activism and philanthropy.

Here are a few benefits of taking smart risks.

Personal and professional growth: Taking risks allows you to challenge yourselves and push beyond your limits, which can lead to personal and professional growth.

Improved problem-solving skills: When you take risks, you often encounter unexpected challenges or setbacks. This can help you to develop your problem-solving skills and to become more resourceful and resilient.

Increased confidence: Successful risk-taking can boost your confidence and help you to believe in yourselves and your abilities.

Greater opportunities: Taking risks can open up new opportunities and doors that you may not have had access to otherwise.

To be a successful risk-taker, it's important to assess and manage risk. One way to do this is to create a risk assessment matrix, which involves identifying the potential risks and evaluating their likelihood and impact. This can help you to prioritize the risks and determine the best course of action. It's also important to have a plan in place to mitigate the risks and to be prepared for any potential challenges or setbacks.

"The biggest risk is not taking any risk. In a world that is changing quickly, the only strategy guaranteed to fail is not taking risks." - Mark Zuckerberg

Overcoming the fear of failure is another important aspect of taking smart risks. Fear of failure is a natural and powerful emotion, and it is important to remember that failure is a necessary part of the learning and growth process. It's okay to be afraid at the moment, and don't let fear hold you back from pursuing your dreams. Instead, focus on the potential benefits of taking risks and try to stay positive and confident.

There are many ways to manage fear and overcome it. One way is to reframe your thoughts and focus on the positive outcomes that can come from taking risks. It can also be helpful to seek support from friends, family, or a mentor, and to remind yourself that you are capable of handling any challenges that may come your way. Some other tactics for managing fear and building confidence include mindfulness techniques, visualization exercises, and challenging negative thought patterns.

Taking smart risks is an essential part of achieving success. By being measured and controlled in your risk-taking, and by overcoming your fear of failure, you can pursue your goals and live fulfilling lives. So, how can you take smart risks in your own life and achieve success like these examples? Here are some tips:

Assess the potential risks and rewards: Before taking a risk, it's important to carefully consider the potential outcomes. Make a list of the potential risks and rewards, and weigh them against each other. This will help you to determine whether the risk is worth taking.

Manage the risk: Once you've decided to take a risk, it's important to have a plan in place to manage it. This may involve identifying potential challenges and developing strategies to overcome them, or it may involve finding ways to mitigate the risks and minimize the potential for negative outcomes.

Seek support: Taking risks can be intimidating, especially if you're doing it alone. It can be helpful to seek support from friends, family, or a mentor, who can provide encouragement and guidance as you pursue your goals.

Be flexible and adaptable: Sometimes, things don't go as planned when you take a risk. It's important to be flexible and adaptable and to be willing to pivot or change course if necessary.

Celebrate your successes: It's important to recognize and celebrate your achievements, no matter how small they may seem. This can help to build confidence and motivation, and can also serve as a reminder of the benefits of taking risks.

So, now it's your turn. Think about an area of your life where you would like to take a risk, and consider how you can apply these tips to make it a smart and successful risk. Remember, risk-taking is an essential part of personal and professional growth, and by taking smart risks, you can achieve your goals and live a fulfilling life.

This is the lover's way and the fifth strategy.

Chapter Summary

- To take smart risks, you will be willing to confront your fears and overcome them.
- The first step towards risk-taking may be the hardest, and it is also the most important.
- Take ownership of your actions and be responsible for the outcomes of your risk-taking.
- Don't let fear hold you back from pursuing your goals and taking smart risks.

In the next chapter, you will learn...

1. The importance of education.
2. Why you should not follow the herd.
3. The benefits of constant learning.

Chapter Six - Lifelong Learning

"A well-educated person has the tools and insight to achieve their goals without infringing on the rights of others."

In this chapter, you will find yourself seeing the world as one. And seeing yourself as an observer in this universe. The art of learning is constantly learning and unlearning.

Ignorance is called the lack of education, and it usually leads to errors and misunderstandings. To thrive in any field, it is essential to educate oneself and acquire the necessary skills and knowledge. Education is not about formal schooling, education is the lifetime process of learning and personal growth.

As Aristotle famously stated, *"The more you know, the more you realize you don't know."* There is always more to learn. It is important to have an open and curious mind.

There are three main types of education: formal, non-formal, and informal. Formal education refers to traditional schooling, where students learn in a structured setting with certified teachers. Non-formal education includes learning opportunities outside of formal schooling, such as workshops and training programs. Informal education refers to the everyday learning that occurs through life experiences, conversations, and exposure to new ideas.

The most effective way to learn is through hands-on experience and applying what one has learned. Simply being told about something is not enough; one must experience it firsthand to truly understand it.

In today's world, there is a phenomenon known as "the herd mentality," where people follow the actions and choices of the majority without questioning whether it is the right decision for them. This can be compared to the metronome synchronization experiment, where all the metronomes eventually tick at the same tempo as the majority. To truly succeed and achieve one's goals, it is crucial to think for oneself and not blindly follow the herd. Blindly accepting trendy, and socially correct doctrine is not the way.

Successful individuals are those who think for themselves, learn from others who have achieved success, continuously improve and adapt to their surroundings, and do not simply follow the path of the majority. They know something that many unsuccessful people do not. They are aware that the path to success involves taking risks and making one's own choices, rather than simply following the herd. If you don't know any successful people, interact with someone who knows successful individuals personally; this increases your chances of success.

To increase your chances of success, it is important to surround yourself with successful individuals or those who have access to successful individuals. The ideas and guidance of the majority, or the "ninety-nine percent," will not likely lead to success, as they are often stuck in the status quo.

"Real knowledge is to know the extent of one's ignorance." - Kǒng Zǐ

Remember that education is a lifelong process and it is never too late to learn and improve. Don't be afraid to challenge yourself and try new things. Seek out new opportunities to learn and grow, and always strive to be the best version of yourself. Always be open to learning and adapting to new things in life.

This is the sixth strategy. It is the scientific way.

Lifestyles I will train and improve upon.	Practical reasons why.	Lifestyles I will unlearn and stop practicing.	Practical reasons why	Action steps
I will become a smarter person.	To be able to get everything I want in this life.	I will stop being a distracted person.	Distraction wastes a lot of my time.	I will focus on one task at a time and practice leveraging my time daily.

Use this format to practice lifelong learning.

CHAPTER SEVEN - FOCUS ON THE FUNDAMENTALS

Every skill that exists is simple to understand. The basis of every skill is in the fundamentals. These are the building blocks and the foundations of perfection. In this chapter, you will appreciate the natural order and patterns behind even the most complex things. From beehives to hundred-story skyscrapers to DNA encoding, to love and romance to building large businesses and achieving superb career success every thing starts from the fundamentals and you will learn these fundamentals this is the way to master strategy.

Cultivate the ability to be present at the moment and the ability to pay attention to yourself. The "ninety-nine percent" often lack this ability, leading to impatience, short attention spans, and costly mistakes.

Instead of looking for shortcuts and quick fixes, it is more rewarding to take the time to learn and understand the core principles of what you do. Many people rush through tasks without fully mastering them, which is why they often fail to achieve their desired outcomes. When you are constantly rushing and worrying about the future, you cannot give your full attention and effort to the present moment. This can also create a false sense of control.

The first thing to master is yourself. Successful individuals tend to pay more attention, they prefer to focus on controlling what they can control. The story of the Tortoise and the Hare teaches, slow and steady wins the race. You are not in direct competition with others or against time, rather, with your negative thoughts and emotions and your inability to patiently master the basics. When you rush through life, you miss out on valuable experiences and opportunities for growth.

If you want to excel in any activity, it is essential to learn and understand its fundamentals. While there are situations where it may seem beneficial to skip the introductions and dive right in, it is usually more beneficial to gain a solid foundation of knowledge before tackling more advanced concepts. Skipping the basics due to laziness or arrogance will only hinder your progress and limit your potential.

There are two types of people in the world. You are either practicing laziness or practicing ambitiousness at any given moment. Those who take the time to learn and master the principles are ambitious. It is important to note that not all hardworking people are ambitious; many people work hard and lack the drive and focus to truly excel and evolve.

Laziness can be a pervasive mindset that affects all aspects of your life and leads to a belief that you are inherently lazy. This is not the truth; laziness is a choice that can be changed. The moment you begin learning and mastering the fundamentals, you are becoming ambitious. Choose to be ambitious and take control of your growth and development.

In everything you do, if you prioritize understanding and mastery over shortcuts, you are already ahead of the curve. This critical practice will increase your chances of living a better life. You become your most beautiful and powerful self when you start this journey, and if you have always been open to learning and using your knowledge and creativity, you are already on the right track. Make the conscious choice to be ambitious and dedicated to continuous learning and growth.

This is the learner's way and the seventh strategy, it is the last of the mainline strategies.

Chapter Summary

- Learn the principles of anything to develop mastery.
- You are either lazy or ambitious; choose who you want to be.
- Start paying more attention.

In the next chapter, you will learn...

1. When war is good and when it is terrible.
2. How to deal with fools.
3. Avoiding compromise.

Phase 2 - The Darker Side

Me: What is the shadow?

Her: The shadow is part of the psyche that contains aspects of oneself that one is **not aware of or does not accept.** It can include both positive and negative traits and may be repressed or denied by the conscious self. The shadow is often associated with Carl Jung's theories and can be seen as the "dark side" of the personality. Engaging with and integrating the shadow can lead to personal growth and self-awareness. In literature and cultural studies, the shadow is often used as a metaphor for the darker, repressed aspects of human nature and society. So it could be seen as an unconscious aspect of the self, which contains qualities and traits that we do not wish to acknowledge or accept.

Me: How do I engage and integrate the shadow?

Her: Here are a few steps that may be helpful in the process:

Increase self-awareness: Start by becoming more aware of your thoughts, feelings, and behaviors. This can be done through practices such as journaling, meditation, or therapy.

Identify the shadow: Look for patterns in your thoughts, feelings, and behaviors that you don't like or don't understand. These may be indications of the shadow.

Reflect on the shadow: Once you have identified the shadow, take time to reflect on it. Consider why you have repressed or denied these aspects of yourself and what they may be trying to communicate to you.

Accept and integrate the shadow: Accept that the shadow is a part of you and try to integrate it into your conscious self. This may involve making changes in your thoughts, feelings, and behaviors, but it can also involve learning to accept and embrace the shadow.

Practice self-compassion: As you engage with your shadow, it can be difficult and uncomfortable, so it's important to practice self-compassion. Be kind and patient with yourself as you navigate this process.

CHAPTER EIGHT - CONFLICT RESOLUTION: NAVIGATING DIFFICULT RELATIONSHIPS

Without knowledge of the beauty that comes from individual differences and appreciation for it, all love feels wanting and all experiences aren't unique. Love is wise, hatred is foolish.

Conflict is an opportunity to evolve, as it can catalyze personal growth and development. However, it is important to recognize and be able to direct and control conflict and to be able to channel that energy in a way that is healthy and constructive. Become more competitive and creative, and approach issues logically.

Do not rush to judgment without considering all the factors, this may lead to misunderstandings and uncontrollable conflict. It is important to nurture and cherish relationships that bring creativity and productivity while being aware of and addressing any negative influences.

Family relationships may be complex, and it may not always be easy to repair damaged bonds. In these cases, it is important to focus on building positive relationships with those you can connect with, and to accept and come to terms with any negative experiences in the past.

It is also important to be mindful of the people you surround yourself with in your work environment. Weaken toxic relationships and cultivate healthy ones, a negative work environment may have a long-lasting impact on your overall well-being. Self-control and the ability to not react impulsively are crucial for effective decision-making and conflict resolution.

In any situation, it is important to identify important facts and ignore unimportant ones and also to stand up for yourself without losing sight of the value of peace. If you find yourself in a situation where conflict is inevitable, be strategic and make sure to emerge victorious. Maintaining inner peace and balance is crucial for optimal performance.

As the saying goes, *"Better to walk alone than with a fool."* Do not let others mistake your kindness for weakness, instead take control of your weaknesses and limitations and turn them into strengths and opportunities.

Providing value and helping others to rise above their limitations is a key step toward self-actualization. In the next chapter, we will discuss the importance of time management and why you procrastinate. You will learn how to use your time more effectively and efficiently to achieve your goals.

This is the way of the fool, the eighth strategy.

CHAPTER NINE - THE ART OF PRIORITIZATION: HOW TO MAKE THE MOST OF YOUR TIME

The beauty of time is its elusiveness. Time is a violent ocean and a calm breeze, time cannot be grasped by the arms, it can only be felt by the senses. Time has no way to be controlled, it is forever free. Time will always pass yet it will never pass away.

This chapter is a dive into the economic value of time. Time is not spent because it is never owned. However, time is experienced constantly and what you do while you experience time in a larger sense is what determines how successful you'll become in the long term. Long-term means a few hundred years at max, time will always continue.

Time is a precious and limited resource. Everyone has the same amount of time each day, and how you choose to use yours has a huge impact on your life. Track how you spend your time. The key strategy here is to spend your time differently, like how successful people spend their time.

Prioritization is about managing time; it is also about using your time the right way. If you are in control of your time you are in control of your life. Proper use of time is often the reason people achieve their goals. It stems from a combination of education and drive, and the only way to cultivate this is to actively work on practicing these behaviors. You can create limitless beliefs and become a most powerful person.

That being said, it's important to take on only the most important activities. Overloading yourself with tasks may lead to procrastination. Instead, focus on a few key tasks each day and make sure you complete them. For the less important tasks, schedule them for a later time or delegate them to someone or something.

The key is to do what you can do now. If a task is not urgent, schedule a specific time to do it and stick to it. Instead of saying, "I'll do it later," say, "I'll do it at 3 pm," or "I'll do it tomorrow at 10 am." This is control and accountability. And if a task is not important, consider finding someone else to do it or simply dump it. Consider becoming familiar with the Eisenhower matrix.

The art of prioritization is a major strategy for achieving your goals, and it's also something you have the power to learn. By being proactive and taking control of your time, you can break free from the cycle of ignorance and procrastination, and start making progress toward the things you want most in life.

This is the master's way, the ninth strategy.

CHAPTER 10 - INVESTING FOR SUCCESS: MAXIMIZING YOUR LIFE

The true purpose of life is to live it to its maximum potential. Express every bit of love with careful consideration. This is the ultimate meaning of this experience. On this journey, everyone deserves complete freedom and you may get it through spiritual enlightenment, with or without having an abundance of money in this world. An abundance of wealth is the way and it is a natural way that may be accomplished by anyone who uses his or her time and available resources in the best possible way.

"The two most powerful warriors are patience and time." - Leo Tolstoy

Continue investing in your future. This chapter is about the importance of investing your time and money wisely. Remember, while money can't buy everything, it can certainly help you achieve many of your goals and dreams.

The real way to financial freedom comes when you leap. Investing in yourself and your personal development is the most important investment you can make. And there are various assets you can invest in that can secure your future and provide financial freedom. Invest with your eyes open. It's important to educate yourself on the best investment opportunities for your specific goals and skillset.

"The two most important days in your life are the day you are born and the day you find out why." - Mark Twain

Investing helps you achieve financial stability and freedom, and it also helps you develop a long-term mindset and allows you to stop chasing money and start living your best life. Smart investors budget their money and include investment as an expense, rather than spending their money on short-term wants. They also invest in what they know in multiple places.

Now is the best time to start investing in your future. Whether it's through investing in your self-development or acquiring assets, the key is to start now and consistently increase by leveraging time and other resources. Have faith in the unknown and love the process. Take control of your future and start investing in your success today.

This is the physical way and the tenth strategy.

CONCLUSION

Every day presents an opportunity to make choices that will shape your future; it is up to you to make the right choices. By staying true to your values and making conscious honest choices, you have the power to achieve anything you desire, in most cases, this is a guarantee that your life will get better. By following the strategies outlined in this book and using your inner creativity, you may develop the skills and mindset to overcome any obstacle and seize the opportunities that come your way. These strategies are here to assist you in doing that; these principles are ideas to help you reach your full potential.

The application of any strategy that you attempt to learn is where magic meets science. Knowing them is the beginning; you should apply them to complete your training. If you begin a habit of always telling the truth, you have to start with yourself. You should be able to tell yourself the truth when you are doing what is suitable for you and when you are not. The first person you should trust is yourself as you apply these principles.

You should go hard on yourself; you should go big every time; you should encourage yourself to do the things you don't want to if you have to do them. Put a little more pressure on yourself. You will learn to think and not to worry. Cause worrying doesn't solve your problems and will only cripple you with anxiety. Think and use your imagination; devise creative ways to overcome your challenges.

Focus on your self-improvement and put in your absolute best in the present. Of course, the part of you that wants to improve is your best self. There is a part of you that wants to get everything, and that is the part that you should feed energy. You should transform the weaker part of yourself so that you will grow. To fully embrace these strategies and achieve your goals, you may need to make some sacrifices. And by choosing to invest in your growth and development, you are taking control of your future and committing to becoming the best version of yourself.

The knowledge which you have gathered when applied with your inner spirit may guide you on your journey and minimize the risk involved. There is no greater glory than the glory you get when you have conquered all your weaknesses. That is the first victory that you should get. In its most simple form, this is living. Living is doing things today better than you did yesterday. Your actions make you who you are. You can choose to take steps that make you a winner. Some steps take you from where you are today to where you want to be tomorrow, and some take you from having nothing to having everything. Some actions do the opposite.

Ignore perfection, you have a body and mind that you can control. You can focus on making progress and becoming the person you want to be. A new identity as trustworthy, honest, and a smart risk-taker? These are questions you should ask yourself as you build your character.

Only concern yourself with whether you are doing what your ideal self would do. Your perfect self would have mastered acquiring everything you want by doing the right things and making the best move. Finding your true identity is the journey of life and self-discovery.

If you want something; see yourself as someone who already has it. Start tracking your choices and their outcomes, recording your thoughts, and ideas quit procrastinating, and leave negativity alone. Embrace your future, where you have everything you want. Embrace your power to shape your own life and create the future you desire. You can take control of your future. Start applying these strategies today and watch your dreams become a reality. No matter where you are in your journey, know that you have the potential to achieve greatness. These strategies will guide you toward the life you deserve.

The final strategy is this; be who you want to become and no one else.

APPENDIX

Thank you for committing to bettering yourself and for choosing this book as a guide. If you found the strategies and principles outlined in these pages to be valuable and are inspired to take action and make positive changes in your life, I encourage you to subscribe to my other works, which can be found at https://linktr.ee/thepowerofaction Here, you will find more resources and tools to help you continue your journey of personal growth and development. Remember, the power to shape your future is in your hands - use it wisely.

ACKNOWLEDGMENTS

First and foremost, I want to thank you for providing me with the opportunity to fulfill this purpose and share my ideas with you. I am grateful for the countless authors, artists, scientists, professionals, entrepreneurs, and creators who have dedicated their lives to understanding the universe and bringing more understanding. I also want to recognize the spiritual leaders and teachers who remind us to live with love and compassion.

I am grateful to the readers who have picked up this book. And of course, I want to express my appreciation to my family, fans, early supporters, enemies, and friends for their unwavering support and encouragement. I thank you all for being a part of this journey.

ABOUT THE AUTHOR

CHINEDU NKWOEMEKA is the founder of Nkwoemeka Corporations, which he founded in 2023. He is also a songwriter and a passionate musical artist. He details helpful ideas for high achievements in his literary debut, "The Power of Action: 11 Strategies for Achieving Your Goals and Living Your Best Life." He has a passion for personal development, creative arts, and technology. Chinedu Nkwoemeka is involved with Amnesty International and is a supporter of the UN World Food Programme. Chinedu enjoys spending time with his friends and family and engaging in his favorite hobbies, such as horse riding and boxing.

NOTES

    <u>*</u> In chess, there are seven types of moves; each of them significantly less powerful than the other, from blunders to brilliant best moves.

* Chronic Narcissism is assumed to be a disorder when a person has an inflated sense of self-importance. The good news is that therapy and meditation help reduce the symptoms.

_*_ The constitution of the Federal Republic of Nigeria considers Perjury a crime punishable by up to fourteen years imprisonment or life imprisonment if the offense was committed to procuring the conviction of another person for an offense punishable with death or imprisonment for life. The criminal code punishes every falsehood, fictitious, fraudulent statement, or any false evidence, whether sworn in any matter within the jurisdiction of the government's executive, legislative, or judicial branch. It is a crime to lie to the government.

* Elite artists usually think with great innovation. They usually also have better semantic and sensory memory, a higher connection to the subconscious, creative thinking, and the ability to perceive or premeditate. These are a few of the mental abilities professional artists develop. While they use these abilities to thrive in the creative arts, everyone can use them in their everyday lives. There are ways to build the artist's mind.

* Your brain is made up of approximately 100 billion neurons that communicate in trillions of connections called synapses, but unlike a hard drive, your brain's storage capacity is unlimited. The human brain can generate up to 23 watts (enough to power a light bulb). The fastest supercomputer made is the Frontier in 2022, reaching a speed of 1.102 exaFlops. An exaFlop is a one thousand quadrillion (one million floating-point calculations per second; since a human brain is not a machine, it is very difficult to calculate precisely how fast it is. Scientists postulate that the human brain operates at over one exaFlop. What makes the human brain so powerful? Efficiency; supercomputers consume thousands of watts of power and are many times larger than a football field. The Frontier occupies 680 m² and takes so much more energy and resources to perform tasks that the human brain will perform after eating a sandwich. The human mind is also capable of emotions, a subconscious, and imagination. Things that no supercomputer can comprehend.

* Various scientists and companies have experimented with integrating technology with human brains for many years. Various types exist that serve multiple purposes, and since the 1960s, the idea has been in discussion. The technology currently serves different purposes; from being used as an address book to being used as a travel card, to being used to store cryptocurrency, or as a payment card, to being used to keep medical records or as a medical identification tag. The future still holds great hope for an all-powerful brain technology integration that will allow the mind to access the internet and the www, enhance the human brain and body capacity, treat diseases, and even achieve symbiosis with artificial intelligence. Such a machine could make the average human what one may call a superhuman. If made possible, people with these computers in their brains could theoretically forget nothing and could access infinite information. This technology is possible. Hopefully, I will be a part of a team that will make it a reality in my lifetime.

* Knowing when and how to position yourself at the right point is a skill that can allow you to benefit from short-term opportunities, it requires foresight. You should understand this concept and know that you are always in transit, on a journey from one point to another, however, keep your sights on the long-term victory.

* Alexander is considered a legend in some Mediterranean cultures. He marched his armies from Greece to Asia Minor, Egypt to Persia, and into the Indus valley, ignoring the negative aspects of his invasions; his willpower, willingness to take risks, and adaptability are traits that everybody should aspire to have.

* Fear is one of the most powerful emotions that a human being can experience. It is a negative emotion, and it can completely incapacitate its victims even while stimulating them. Fear has different forms and comes from various sources; sometimes, your worries are internal and self-inflicted; other times, your fears are external, meaning coming from outside sources and other people. You will be able to face your fears squarely and convince yourself that you can overcome them because you can and in most cases these fears aren't even real. You will be able to control your mind and avoid the negative influence from the outside that will try to control you. Your now-conquered fears will gain you confidence.

* The crowd could be any majority, a group of people, a popular idea, or a style of doing things. It's always a good idea to think twice before following the crowd, do not blame them. Sometimes they may be correct, other times, they may be wrong. The mistake people make is thinking that because everybody is doing it, then they should do it also, or it's the right thing or the "in thing" to do, following trends or riding waves, it all means the same thing, idly going with the popular opinion based on sentiment because it is popular, not because it is based on fact or accurate thinking.

* The metronome synchronization experiment is a simple experiment where the person experimenting places a group of metronomes on a board and places this board on rollers. She swings all the metronomes at random. At first, they're all ticking at different speeds, after a while, the metronomes synchronize because their forces either cancel out or add up together, bringing them closer to the group. By the end of the experiment, all the metronomes are swinging at the same tempo. This experiment is interesting because it proves that, under fluid conditions, different bodies tend to behave like each other, which is also how society tends to behave.

At birth, everyone is genetically unique. Still, after interacting with the community, they start to identify with groups like mosques, schools, political parties, teams, or even people with similar interests. So they adapt to fit into the group. Your behavior becomes identical within each group you are in, and the people in those groups interact with people in other groups to form an even larger group. Those people interact with people from other large groups to create an even larger group. Still, members interact with each other and cross between groups. Incidentally, individuals behave similarly to the people and groups they interact with online and face-to-face, adopting similar ideas and behavioral and thinking patterns.

* The story of the Tortoise and the Hare is famous; it is derived from ancient folklore and credited to Aesop from his book, Fables. The story goes like this; a Hare was making fun of the Tortoise for being so slow, so the Tortoise challenged the Hare to a race to prove who was faster. The Hare agreed, hoping to embarrass the Tortoise. As soon as the race started, the Hare dashed ahead, the Tortoise began sauntering. Before long, the Hare was already far out of sight; to show how ridiculous it was for the Tortoise to challenge him, he lay down beside the course to take a nap until the Tortoise should catch up to him. The Tortoise, meanwhile, kept going slowly and steadily and eventually reached where the Hare was and passed him. The Hare kept sleeping. When the Tortoise was near the finish line, the Hare woke up and ran as fast as he could, but he could not overtake the Tortoise in time. The Tortoise won the race.

There is another version where the Tortoise tricked the Hare by working with all his family members to stand at different intervals on the course so that no matter how fast the Hare ran, he would always see a Tortoise ahead of him. In the original version, the Tortoise didn't win because of trickery, he won because of steadiness and persistence. The Hare lost even with his natural talent because of foolishness and overconfidence. Being intelligent and disciplined is essential, with or without natural talent.

* To see yourself as a student means always being eager to learn and not being too proud to admit when you are wrong. That is the only proper way to become a master. Every great master was once a great student. Young children are always curious, they want to discover the world in great detail; their open-mindedness is their greatest strength and one of the sources of their creativity; it is very valuable.

* A family is an organization. The family is a level of government more diminutive than the local government, it is usually without a written constitution. All nations are a giant conglomerate of families. Thousands of years ago, the first tribes only comprised a few families, maybe only one large family, later more families came together and grew larger to form villages, then they grew to become towns and states.

The smallest family unit in modern society is the nuclear family, this is the most important and indirectly the most powerful level of government on an individual, it is certainly the most influential. The family molds the ideas and behavior of most people. A solid and stable family unit will most likely create a strong and durable individual, an unstable family will do the opposite. If you trace it back, most of the ideas you have today are rooted in your family's philosophies, with natural deviations resulting from modernization, socialization, and your personal experiences. A weak nation often results from a fragile family system, and a strong nation results from stronger family systems and ideas. To change society, you will have to start with your family.

* Yelling, fighting, or becoming overly emotional is hardly the right way to handle any situation. Self-control is vital; without it, you may not realize your dreams and goals. As soon as you lose self-control, you should detach from the event and your personal feelings and see the bigger picture. Self-control is the best way to maintain a stable and strong relationship.

* Scheduling tasks is personal and depends on your workload and your mental and physical capacity; it is also subjective, and the most important thing is having your day planned in such a way that you are most effective. Scheduling is about conserving energy, avoiding burnout, and putting in your best with minimal effort.

* Money is a tool. The infinite chaos in the universe isn't controlled by money. Theoretically, you can acquire everything that can be sold and bought with money. Although you could love money, money remains a means of exchange. It will always go to those who provide the most value in the system.

* Everyone should acquire the right assets that fit their financial plan and build themselves up personally.

QUOTABLE

- Imagination is dynamic power.

- Those with the best ideas win.

- Imagination is power. Creativity is power.

- Seek abundance.

- Living is doing things today better than you did yesterday.

*Download these resources here.

1. Life Plan Template.
2. List of ideas for your personal development.

https://linktr.ee/thepowerofaction

The page will be regularly updated with new resources and improvements to the old ones.

Notebook